The Original

Enjoy beer with cheese

FSC
www.fsc.org
MIX
Papier aus verantwortungsvollen Quellen
Paper from responsible sources
FSC® C105338

Harald Müller

Original German title:
Genuss mit Bier und Käse,
Genuss mit allen Sinnen.

The „slightly" different experience!
A guide to beer and cheese tasting.

How to prepare and host your own beer and
cheese tasting.

Bibliografische Information der Deutschen Nationalbibliothek:
Die Deutsche Nationalbibliothek verzeichnet diese Publikation in der Deutschen Nationalbibliografie; detaillierte bibliografische Daten sind im Internet über http://dnb.de und https://portal.dnb.de/opac.htm abrufbar.

2. Auflage überarbeitet (früher bei TwentySix.de)

© 2022 Harald Müller

Herstellung und Verlag:
BoD – Books on Demand,
Norderstedt
Deutschland/Germany

ISBN: 978-3-756-84039-7

Bibliographic information from the German National Library:
The German National Library lists this publication in the German National Bibliography; Detailed bibliographic data are available on the Internet at http://dnb.de and https://portal.dnb.de/opac.htm

2nd Edition

© 2022 Harald Müller

Production and publishing:
BoD – Books on Demand, Norderstedt

content

Preface
How this book project was born!
Dear reader, beer lover, cheese lover,

Good food has always been important to me.

My first experience with beer and cheese was a tasting in a small brewery in San Francisco. That was in 2005.

I think it was the „Thirsty Bear Brewing Company ". I had a „flight "– a variation of three different beers in small glasses and the matching cheese on the side. I was flashed.
Since then, I do my own beer and cheese tastings and decided to write a little book about my experiences.

I would like to share what I have learned and enjoyed over the last few years in a way that you can host and enjoy your own "casual tasting".

I wish that you enjoy it and use it, expand it, share it, and simply have a lot of fun with it.

Oh, by the way, I am the one who translated the German version into English. I have tried to make it as easy to read as possible and since there are beers and cheese styles that are German/European I have tried to write it from a global point of view. This is not just a translation of words but also a translation of the idea. Please enjoy this experience.

Beer and cheese! Does that work? Wine and cheese have often been paired and can be found on menus and on party tables. Some connoisseurs believe that finding the right beer to go with cheese is a bit difficult, but once you have grasped the idea that I share with you in this book, you will see that it is very easy to repeat and adopt for your own purposes.

You will look at every cheese counter and even every cheese variation with "beery" eyes and then search for the right beer. You will see each beer shelf in the beverage department with different eyes. If you do, I would be delighted.

I hope you can enjoy the idea and soon host your own beer and cheese tasting.

I would like to point out that I do not cover the craft beers in detail. Why? Well, I think it is just impossible to always find the right companion due to huge variety of craft beers and the many types of cheese with their individual tastes. But with the tools and methods I offer you find your own way.

In addition, what is the point of recommending a craft beer and cheese to go with if you do not have the opportunity to get hold of that beer or cheese?

In this book I am referring to the "common" beers and their typical properties such as taste, smell and appearance and the cheese that goes with it (in my opinion), so that you can adopt the idea of beer and cheese tastings and create your own little adventure.

Every good craft beer pub and restaurant has its own recommendations for dishes and beers to match.

This means that the beer that is recommended on the menu has been chosen to give you as a guest the best experience. Due to the many different craft beer variations, it is difficult to make a fair or precise recommendation.

In any case, if you try out the idea of this book, you will get a feeling of what goes together, and if you discover a craft beer or a new cheese you will get an idea and find a suitable combination.

Nevertheless, at the end of the book, for the sake of completeness, I will briefly address some of the properties of craft beers and try inspiring you to come up with your own ideas for your beer-cheese combinations.

My goal is: if you go through and try the samples that I am offering here, you will end up having a good gut feeling of choosing your favourite beer or cheese to then plan your own tasting.

In the appendix you will find a shopping list that you can use and expand accordingly.

You do not have to be a beer sommelier or cheese aficionado to enjoy!

It is easy to enjoy and to find your own matches and never stop experimenting. Enjoy with family and friends, simply improve your quality of life, at least a little bit.

A few basics

The beer!

During the brewing process, malt and water are mixed to a mash and then heated through several temperature levels to activate enzymes, which then support the necessary processes to produce a mash that contains enough maltose for fermentation. Yeast is added after cooling to convert the sugar into alcohol.

The sugar content is measured in "°Plato" and denotes the original wort.
In the old days hops was primarily used to make the beer stable for storage and for the journey to the colonies. Hops is now also used for taste and flavour, fresh of the fields, dried, as pellets or as concentrate. There are quite a few different types of hops on the market that are used to add bitterness, flavour and aroma.

Barley, wheat, and other grains are used in different ratios for brewing, depending on the type of beer.

There are also many different yeast strains that are used depending on the type of beer and fermentation temperature - top-fermented

or bottom-fermented - taste, clarity, and degree of fermentation.
Since the water is the most controlled food item, it may still be processed by the breweries to ensure consistent quality.

That was the short version just to give you a quick glimpse into the brewing process! There are also great books that give you a detailed understanding of the brewing process.

The cheese!

Cheese maker mainly use cow's milk, sheep's milk, goat's milk, and buffalo milk.

By heating the milk and adding enzymes the curd is created which, depending on the type of cheese, is then further processed, and later refined, finished, and aged.

Milk for raw milk cheese is not pasteurized, i.e., not heated above 72 ° - 75 ° C / 161° - 167° F and remains below 50 ° C / 122° F during processing.

Pregnant women should therefore not eat raw milk cheese, as it can contain bacteria that may be harmful to their health. If you are pregnant, please ask your doctor before you eat raw milk cheese.

The production of beer and cheese is a very clean process and unclean working methods are reflected directly in the product.

Again, just a brief overview. More on this later.

What to expect!

By pairing beer with cheese, we start with the "light" beer and a "light" cheese and increase according to style, taste, alcohol content of the beer and character, richness, and age of the cheese.

Janet Fletcher writes in her book about beer and cheese that the interaction is like a tennis match: if the players are of a similar format, then the game is more exciting, more balanced, and easier to watch.

A ricotta with a light pale ale or a fresh buffalo mozzarella with a Kriek, the Belgian cherry beer, makes more sense than pairing a light cheese with a powerful stout or a Doppelbock with a simple cream cheese.

But you can also serve a cheesecake with a Kriek for dessert. In any case, I hope you enjoy it.

Our senses make sense!

Take a look!

"There is no second chance for the first impression!" - anonymous –

The appearance of food and drinks has a direct influence on our selection. That is why we sometimes have a hard time in front of a huge buffet and cannot decide where to strike first.

Do you eat with your eyes? Well, we first perceive food with the eye, and if something looks appealing, then the first step has already been taken. Regardless of whether a salad is garnished with tomato, bell peppers, chickpeas, asparagus, or egg, it looks like a "rainbow", and this is good for the eye, so it is good for us as viewers.

As with every meal, we try and make the prepared look nice on the plate – the right plate, some garnish, even if it is just the parsley in the soup - and it looks fine. Numerous studies prove this.

For the tasting I use simple (0.1 litre/approx. 3,5 ounces) champagne glasses, small plates with muffin or cupcake liners for the cheese. It looks nice and produces little waste. There are no limits to your creativity.

The Beer!

Beer and cheese are also rated by colour.

The beer colour according to the EBC
(EBC = European Brewery Convention)

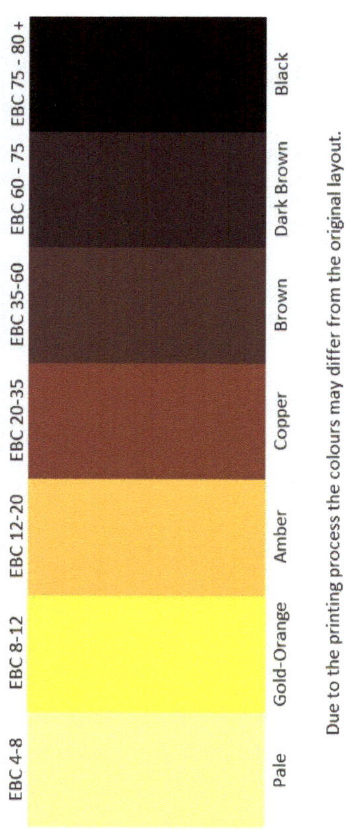

Pale: Pilsner, Pale Ale, Kölsch, Bock,

Gold-Orange: Märzen, Pilsner, Wheat

Amber: Alt, Bock, Trappist, Pilsner

Copper: Red-Beer, Craft beer

Brown: Bock, Brune (Belgium style), Stout

Black: Stout, Imperial Stout

As you already know, the colours of the beer types overlap. A bock is not always dark, and a Pilsner is not always just bright or pale.

Fruit beers and fruit beer cocktails have their own colour nuances due to the addition of syrup or fruit juice extract from pink to dark red, greenish, and bluish or eggplant - depending on the fruit and the brewing/bottling/mixing process.

Clear (mostly cold filtered) or cloudy is easy to differentiate and is also part of the beer type. Cloudy substances not only make the beer look good according to the type, but also give the beer taste and the corresponding mouthfeel.

The "additives" like syrup or juice concentrate can also make a beer look more appealing and certainly add taste.
The head (foam) of the Pilsner, a feature not to be underestimated, is also an indicator of correct pouring.

The foam stability is important and is often destroyed by a dry, unclean and/or dusty glass. Always rinse the glass with cold water prior to tapping or pouring the beer.

The beer colour is mainly regulated by the malt and the boiling time. Some malts make the beer light pale others add a golden yellow tone, depending on the recipe of course. Toasted and / or coloured malt is used to make darker beers.

If a batch is boiled for a longer time (boiling time is usually 60-90 minutes), it can also become darker. With the common beers from large breweries, this is of course precisely regulated to ensure consistent quality.

The right glass helps the beer to present itself accordingly and to develop its typical aromas.

The shape of the right glass should also not be underestimated, as it brings out the colour, foam, and aroma much better. But do not worry, you do not have to buy an extra set for every beer.

The beer glass: a slim Pilsner glass or a tulip formed Pilsner glass with a golden rim looks classy. A "Willi-Becher" mug, the pendant to a pint glass is a bit simpler and a beautifully shaped wheat beer glass has something elegant about it.
A Trappist glass impresses with its very elaborate design and looks appealing even without its contents. For craft beers, there are many special glasses according to the beer style or type.

As far as the drinking temperature is concerned, you will find the recommended drinking temperature printed on the label of many bottles. I cool the beer to about 8 ° - 10 ° C / 45° - 50° F.
It will warm up by itself and when I have guests or am a guest, the beer always has time to adjust to the room temperature. You will be amazed what an affect a few degrees will have on the aroma and taste.

The Cheese!

Certain types of cheese always have their typical colour and consistency. When you are at the cheese counter, pay attention to the shapes, colours, and packaging.
Proper presented and the cut surface in the right light whets your appetite. The content of water influences taste, colour, consistency of cheese.

For example, the information on the cheese in Germany is often displayed as "50% Fett i. Tr.", sometimes also "at least 50% Fett i. Tr." means the fat content without the water (Fat in dry matter)!

If you would be able to remove 100% of the water from the cheese you would basically end up with fat, protein, salt, vitamins, enzymes, milk sugar and lactic acid.

A few samples and colours:

bright white: Picandou, buffalo mozzarella, curd cheese or Mascarpone

Yellow shades: Gouda, Edam, and other semi-hard cheeses

Light brown rind and yellow on the inside: smoked mozzarella or a Morbier.

Outside reddish to orange: Munster, Romadur or Limburger

Dark brown: Salers

Red brown: Castelmagno

Golden brown: Provolone Valpadana.

Blue-gray rind: Chabichou du Poitou, or goat cheese rolled in ashes

Blue cheese (yellowish): Gorgonzola and Blue Stilton

White, velvet, soft rind: Brie and Camembert

Standard-Cheese-Colours

Cheese comes in shapes from square to round, as a roll, loaf, or pyramid, in the shape of a flower, wrapped in leaves, placed in a brine - the shapes are limitless, and the cheese makers are very creative.

The cut surface of the cheese, the structure, the distribution of the bubbles as well as the distribution of mould spores in blue cheese become visible.
Uniform colouring is also assessed as a criterion. The rind of some cheeses is eatable, others rather not. Just ask the personnel. But since we are focusing on the beer and cheese pairing, this should be enough for now.

Often the cheese are the result of maturation and refinement. Partly by chance, or on purpose, partly through trial and error and of course for marketing reasons.

In addition, there is the packaging in foil, fine wax paper, wooden boxes, stoneware and provided with all sorts of labels, which is sometimes also important to prove the origin. Speaking of packaging, remove the cheese from the packaging at least 30 Minutes before tasting. It needs to breeeeeeathe!

The Origin!

There are protected designations of origin of the EU: "PDO", "protected designation of origin" and "g.t.S.", for "guaranteed traditional speciality".

Incidentally, this not only applies to cheese or beer, but also to many other foods.

This has its price, but we as consumers should be interested in where our food really comes from.

In Great Britain, the abbreviation PDO (Protected Designation of Origin) applies, in France among other things AOC (Appellation d'Origine Contrôlée) and in Italy DOP (Denominazione d'Origine Protetta).

There are also many more regional names and descriptions within a country or area.

The three types of smelling: nasal - retro nasal - trigeminal smell.

When we hold food to our nose and take in the scent, this is called "pro-nasal" smelling. If we have the food in our mouth, the smell also reaches the nasal mucosa via the pharynx and is registered there "retro nasally".

A pungent odour is like a pain stimulus that is perceived through the nerve tracts of the "trigeminus nerve". That should suffice as a little insight and is also the reason why I am describing the common beers and natural cheeses in this book, not herbal cheeses or flavoured cheeses. Otherwise, pairing it with a beer would be difficult if not impossible in my opinion.

Before the tasting or just like that, you can also do smelling exercises. Simply smell different spices, herbs or fruits and try to recognize the nuances and thus become more and more sensitive to differentiating different smells. It's fun and once you've started, you're always more excited to explore new impressions and combinations.

A Mozzarella di Bufala or Burrata, a subspecies of Mozzarella, usually smells very buttery, creamy or like fresh milk. Please, I'm talking about real mozzarella made from buffalo milk or the Burrata with the cream filling.

Stilton, a completely different consistency, usually smells fruity, nutty and buttery and the older it gets a bit piquant - spicy.
This is one of the reasons why this cheese is often referred to as "The King of English Cheeses".

Together with the right beer, another unique aroma develops in the mouth, which is mainly perceived retro nasal. That is exactly what I would like to bring you closer to: An unforgettable culinary experience with beer and cheese.

The aromas that we perceive will go into our subconscious and are there "processed". That will protect us from ingesting something spoiled.

Of course, we see what we eat or drink first, but the smell is the sense that protects us from bad food and is the first thing that is imprinted in our subconscious.

If a beer is old or has been stored incorrectly, it can become sour. Believe me, you will smell it before you taste it.

If you store your beer correctly and do not let it get old, you do not need to have the negative experience of an old or spoiled beer. Simple.

The beer aroma in traditional beers is largely determined by the addition of hops during the brewing process. In craft beers, hops are also added during or after the fermentation process.

The beer aroma ranges from tangy/dry to grassy for normal beers and fruity and flowery for craft beers brewed with a single hop variety or a mixture of hop varieties. There are lemon notes, tangerines, chocolate, mocha and many more.

High-proof beers often have a vinous smell. For example, a Doppelbock, Trappist or a "Barley Wine" has such a typical smell.

This may seem a little strange to you at the moment, but with the right cheese it is also a pleasure not to be missed.

If you are interested in beer, you don't have to be a sommelier, but you can use the "Beer Aroma Guide" to find out more. This is a coloured, printed round table with the taste and smell nuances that play a role in beer tasting.

The Beer Aroma Guide shows the different nuances from "aromatic, fragrant - spicy/winey" to "sulphurous, sulphide like - sulphur vapour/rotten eggs" and in between from "apple and acetone" to "fruity, flowery" to "rancid butter and sweat"! Roast aromas, yeast aromas (banana in Hefeweizen), hop aromas (hop bitter), grassy, nutty, and some more.

I would like to point out that the use of the Aroma Guide is not easy and not really necessary for a beer-cheese tasting, but it can help to discover and classify certain smells and tastes.

An aroma guide can always help you when it comes to food and is a good addition for you as a connoisseur to train your senses. I always have it with me during my tastings and often look into positively astonished faces.

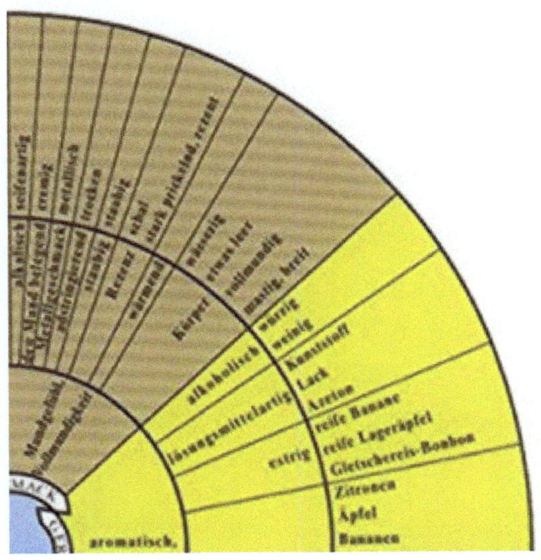

The cheese!

When tasting cheese, there are similar criteria to those as for beer, which are of course also standardized.

As already mentioned, the smell in general goes directly into our subconscious, is "stored" there and influences the handling of food, the environment and our fellow human beings. "I like that smell!" does not only apply to cheese!

Scent, texture and taste are some of the tasting criteria. For the scent, depending on the type of cheese and its origin, a distinction is made between the properties of "sour - milky - yeasty / fermented - creamy" and classified in terms of intensity from "not available" to "very strong".

There is also "aromatic - earthy - fruity - grassy".

Sweet, salty, sour and bitter are known to everyone. We were taught that in school.

The tongue and what we once learned.

Earlier:
In some books the old variant of the taste distribution on the tongue is still shown.
This means that the tip of the tongue registers salty, the area just behind it is sweet, the side edges (left and right) are sour and the rear area is bitter.
By the way, "spicy" is not a taste, but a pain stimulus.

Today:
According to the sources I know, it is more as shown in the pictures (symbolic), the areas tend to overlap, but do have some weighting.

sweet

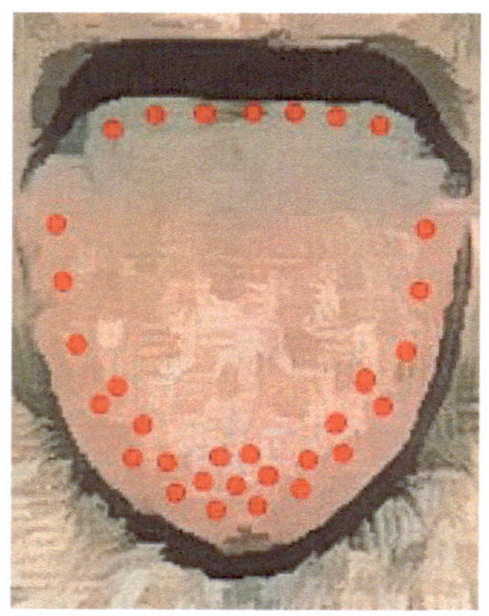

sour

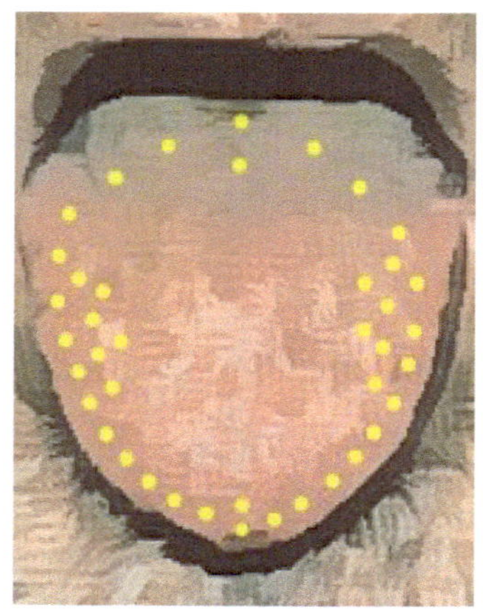

bitter

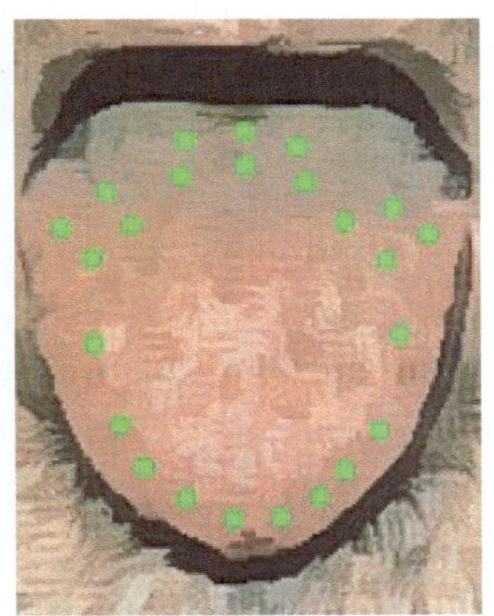

salty

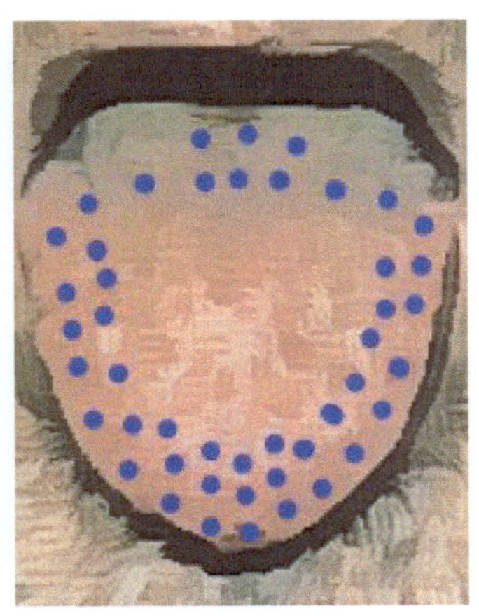

We have about 2000 taste buds on the tongue. Half wall papillae and half fungal papillae. Each of these papillae has between 10-15 taste cells that have a lifespan of about 10 days. So if you burn your tongue, you should get better after a few days.

The 4 main flavours are distributed all around the tongue and each have a tendency or the areas are more or less intense: 'sweet' a little more at the tip; 'Sour' a little more on the side; 'Bitter' more in the back and 'salty' in the front and sides, but less in the back.

The middle area is also not without taste buds. Certainly we taste a little of the main flavours there too, but this area mainly takes up the fifth taste!

Umami stands for hearty, "meaty" or also tasty. Dried tomatoes, simply baked as a snack or in a ciabatta, soy sauce and fish sauce also bring this umami taste into our dishes.

Umami is a natural flavour enhancer!
If you enter "umami" in your Internet search engine, you will currently (2022) find over 30 million entries in less than a second. In 2015 it was "only" just over 2 million.
Umami spice mixes are available in different textures. Ground for sprinkling or as a paste. Vegan variants are also available as well as recipes to make "umami" yourself!

Mouthfeel: "sucking" the cheese and "slurping" the beer.

Just like tasting tea, coffee or wine, it is important to get air (oxygen and other constituents of the air) into your mouth and nose so that it can develop its aromas.
Don't worry, we're not slurping ourselves into nirvana.
By allowing the cheese to melt in the mouth, it warms up and spreads out and you can taste the typical nuances. Try it: you will be amazed.

Body and mouthfeel!

The brewing process, i.e. the pouring process, controls, among other things, the body of the beer. In my opinion, it is not important whether the beer is top-fermented or bottom-fermented for pairing with the cheese, because it is the combination that makes the taste pleasant for the connoisseur.
Especially the maltose-rest during the brewing process, influences the body and richness through temperature and time.
A longer maltose-rest reduces the fullness and vice versa. The alcohol content is also determined by the recipe and the brewing process.

Why is this important? It is simply part of the recipe for the style/type of beer that is brewed.
In addition, the water used for brewing is constantly monitored and sometimes treated to ensure consistent quality.

The "original gravity" indicates the sugar content before fermentation. During fermentation, this sugar is mainly converted into alcohol and displayed percentages. (% Alcohol by Volume)

The mouthfeel, the first sip, the first - initial taste, some carbonic acid...

Do you remember the term "retro nasal"? We do not only taste when we put something in our mouth, but also smell through the interplay of the pharynx and the nasal mucous membrane.

In the case of cheese, the mouthfeel, and in the case of beer, the taste are some of the components that allow us to decide between pleasant and unpleasant.

Beer tasting!

Taste, mouthfeel, richness. The glass on the lips and the first sip in the mouth and on the tongue. We can also let the foam develop its aroma first in the mouth. Sometimes the beer foam seems more bitter to us than the beer itself, because it came into contact with oxygen beforehand and the aromas can develop differently than the beer itself. Or, it is just the hops. The beer in your mouth, hits the tongue and the frontal mucous membrane of the mouth.
Freshness - tingling, acidity - sour - bitter or stale, stale,
soft - velvety, are some of the properties that you can taste.

The beer aromas are now doing the magic. The tongue and the oral mucosa come into contact with the drink. Now you can taste the sweetness and bitterness that unfolds in the mouth. If you keep your mouth closed and your cheeks inflated a little like rinsing while brushing your teeth, then you have the entire mouth in contact with the beer and that is the transition to the final or finish taste.

You now swallow the beer. If you also try to exhale slowly through your nose, these aromas will be more intensely absorbed through the pharynx and perceived more intensely. Now the tongue perceives 'sweet', 'malty', 'sour', 'bitter', 'umami'. If the beer suits your taste, you'll want more.

One of the most important factors that influence the taste of the cheese is the feeding of the animals. The milk treatment, the cheese maker and the maturation or refinement add the special characters to the cheese.
Before you put the cheese in your mouth. please make sure that the rind edible. With some cheeses, the rind is edible but not necessarily a pleasure and should therefore be removed. The best thing is to ask about it when you go shopping for cheese.

The mouthfeel of cheese is often decisive for its enjoyment. Many people cannot eat yogurt or cottage cheese, as the consistency alone causes discomfort. Adjust your cheese selection accordingly.

A mozzarella is slightly firm to creamy, a brie is rather doughy and velvety and a parmesan from firm to crumbly, as it is not cut, but broken.

You remember the flavours: sweet, salty, umami, sour, bitter. Then there is the mouthfeel. With cream cheese, for example, we can feel the creamy consistency. The doughy to firm consistency of semi-hard cheese and firm to crumbly consistency of hard cheese.

With some very mature hard cheeses, you may feel a crystalline structure in your mouth, as if they are small grains or particles that dissolve when you suck them. Don't worry, this is intentional and definitely a quality feature.

The fat content also plays a role, as fat is an essential flavour carrier. Since we do not consume a huge amount of cheese during the tasting, we can also use a little more fat here.

Now a little more about the taste of different cheeses.

Cream cheese, e.g. Ricotta has mild, lemon-like fresh notes, a Mascarpone is more sweet and creamy and a young feta has slightly spicy notes with a little acidity.

Ripe cream cheese tastes creamy and milky at first. The Sainte-Maure de Touraine, rolled in ashes, the typical Chèvre flavours with nutty, slightly spicy and lemony nuances, is always an experience.

Soft cheese, depending on the milk, tastes like mushrooms, almonds and ammonia due to the ripening process, like Brie or Camembert, with a smooth to creamy and velvety mouthfeel.

Semi-hard cheese indicates a buttery, soft and sometimes meaty taste. Red smear cheese with a slightly sour taste and doughy consistency.

Hard cheese tastes slightly hot to buttery, sometimes a little sweet like caramel like a Manchego. As these cheeses mature, fruity notes can be added. The Parmigiano-Reggiano has a fresh pineapple flavour with little heat. A Grana Padano surprises with additional dried fruit notes.

For some of you the **Blue cheeses** may not be the best choice at first, especially when they have melted on bread or pasta. Blue cheeses can taste spicy and aggressive when young and then changes over time into buttery, nutty with cocoa notes is a pleasure.

A Roquefort has more spicy, strong aromas, while the Gorgonzola tastes hot, spicy and less salty.

In addition to viewing, smelling and tasting cheese, the consistency, the hand feeling, is also part of the tasting process. Please remember that this is not about tasting beer **or** cheese, but rather about tasting beer **with** cheese.

The tasting event!

Here are 6 beer-cheese pairings as I offer them at my events.
You can adapt these for your own tasting event or combine them your way and I am sure that you will get a good feeling about what goes well together.

In a normal tasting, I offer only 5 or 6 pairs. In this case, you have the option of picking the right cheeses and beers from the range depending on the availability of the cheeses and beers.
More than 5 or 6 pairs may be to much.

First things first!

The glass is rinsed with cold water to remove any dust or soap residue. I use champagne glasses for about 0.1 litres approx. 3-4 oz of beer. It is best to pour the beer so that it foams.

This is how oxygen comes into contact with the beer and the aromas can develop. I like to place the cheese in a muffin paper on a small plate or bowl.

The guest can nibble the cheese several times and drink the beer in small sips.

It is served!

You can serve all types of cheese but let them breathe. In any case, take the cheese out of the packaging beforehand and, if possible, do not store it in the same room in which your tasting takes place. As already mentioned, let the beer also come to temperature.

We look at the beer ... cloudy, clear, light, dark, golden, reddish, amber-coloured, black.

We smell the beer.... yeasty, hoppy, fruity. Use the previous chapters again for help. The aroma wheel can now also be used, or just rely on your nose and your palate.

We take a small sip of beer in our mouths....

We look at the cheese, ... white, yellowish, golden yellow, streaked with mould, bubbles.

We smell the cheese, ... light, aromatic, penetrating, vinous, ... bite off a piece, suck the cheese, ... velvety, crumbly, greasy, fresh, ... let it melt on your tongue.

We sip on, sip on the beer, let it unfold in the mouth. What is on your mind besides the beer? The initial taste, sweetness, tartness, bitterness, tingling on the tongue, sour -
Another sip, drink ... rinse in your mouth, swallow the beer – finish and enjoy!

Tat-ta-taaaa!

What always works!

Samples, which simply everyone can enjoy!

The pairings described here are simple and easy for you to try.
Of course, there are many variations and strong fluctuations within one type of cheese and beer. I am certain that you will enjoy the pairings and grasp the idea.

Let's start ...

Fruity and tender

The beer: a Kriek, a Belgium Cherry beer, light, sweet, slightly sour on your palate, approx. 4% Alcohol (or a Cassis Lambic Beer). If you can't get the cherry beer, who should stop you from mixing a light lager or ale with some cherry syrup yourself? But please not too much syrup, otherwise it will be too sweet and "sticky".

The cheese: a buffalo mozzarella. The real stuff. You will quickly notice that this mozzarella has little to do with the cheap product from the discounter. The smell and taste of the buffalo mozzarella is reminiscent of "old milk": not sour, but ripe buttery, mild and slightly sweet. (A fresh yogurt would also fit here or something with Panna Cotta or Mascarpone for dessert.)

Yeasty and delicate

A wheat beer, I prefer the German Weizen, cool and fresh, soft in taste, smells a bit like ripe bananas, goes well with a not too spicy feta. Try your local Weizen but please do not add the Lemon. Choose one with a real wheat taste.

The cheese: From goats or sheep's milk e.g. a feta Xenia, a bit sour and slightly salty, which causes tingling on the tongue and the palate. When it melts on the tongue, it is soft and velvety on the finish.

Blonde and smooth

The beer: A Kölsch, with 4.8% Alcohol, still quite low in alcohol, a Märzen (seasonal) or a Leffe Blonde will work wonderful here too. Many breweries offer a Kölsch style beer. A pale ale or bitter will work here as well.

The cheese: A Brie, not too ripe, or a Camembert, is a great accompaniment here. Both are soft in consistency, velvety-creamy but not too creamy in the mouth and with slight mushroom aromas. Those who prefer a firmer consistency can try a Comte or a young Gouda.

Hoppy and aromatic

The beer: a good Pilsner, e.g. a Pilsner Urquell, Budweiser, or similar with a pleasant aroma and the typical bitterness.

The cheese: a Munster with the typical "red smear" (Rotschmiere) on the outside. Usually, it smells stronger than it tastes.
Strong, yeasty and slightly blossomy, it would also go well with a wheat beer, but I would enjoy it with a good Pilsner, as the bitterness of the beer and the "red smear" go well together.

Strong and ripe

The beer: A strong Amber, a Trappist with a strong aroma and an alcohol content of just over 5.5% Alcohol. not only smells rich and strong, but also tastes hearty and has few bitter notes. Try a Samuel Adams Lager.

The cheese: a goat cheese rolled in ashes, e.g. a Gour Noir, well matured, velvety on your tongue and with the typical strong and ripe and rich taste. The Scamorza, a smoked mozzarella also tastes great with it.

Intense and delicate

The beer: A Barley Wine or Imperial Stout, a Quadrupel or Maredsous (> = 10% Alc.). Strong, aromatic nose, full bodied and somewhat sweetish strong in the taste. Don't go to bitter, rather rich and strong.

The cheese: a rich blue cheese, the Stilton. The "King of English Cheeses".

There aren't many dairies that make this wonderful blue cheese. Suck the Stilton, smell and sip the beer. You will understand.

It is difficult to choose an alternative, but in an "emergency" you can go with a Roquefort or Bergader.

My little helpers:

Small porcelain bowls, coasters, or espresso plates (1 per person)

Muffin baking paper (1 per person per cheese)
Glasses (0.1l or 3-4 oz. champagne glasses), napkins
Cutting board, cooking gloves, cheese knifes (for soft cheese, hard cheese, blue cheese)

Bottle opener / corkscrew (large Kriek bottles have a cork, sometimes a crown cap and a cork)

Your shopping list for 4 people could look like this:

approx. 0.75l / a pint and a half per beer style should be enough. Remember, this is a tasting. The party starts later.

For the cheese, calculate 40g / a heaped table-spoon per cheese style is sufficient for the tast-ing.

It goes without saying that you buy high qual-ity cheese as already mentioned.

Suggestions for your future pairings

You have noticed that I always start with the beer. That is probably because I find it easier to pair the cheese with the beer than to find the beer that accompanies the cheese.

Due to variations of the cheese styles some of them appear several times on the list and "overlap" the beer styles a few times.

I could and would not draw a strict line and challenge your creativity to let your taste run wild.

The list is by no means complete, but it does give you an overview and an idea of what might go together in your future tastings.

If you are planning a tasting, please purchase good quality cheese. Slices of processed cheese wrapped in foil may belong on a burger and the super cheap Camembert in the rucksack, and only for an emergency.

Kriek, Belgian cherry beer, Morte Subite, Lindemanns. Floris Fraise or Framboise, Leffe Ruby, ... these beers have an alcohol content between 3.5 - 4.5% by Vol.	Mozzarella, the real buffalo mozzarella or a burrata. I do not have many alternatives here, but a cheesecake for dessert is also compatible with a Kriek. Mascarpone (as part of a dessert), panna cotta, yoghurt, ...
Wheat/Weizen from Erdinger, Paulaner are available around the world, or choose your favorite wheat beer, a Belgian Witbier, ... If you choose a Wheat make sure that it does have a typical banana aroma!	Feta, as long as it is the real feta, ... a slightly more "mature" cream cheese, fresh goat cheese, (herbed cream cheese)
a Kölsch style beer (top fermented but then treated like a lager), a regular lager, a Blonde or Märzen,	A young brie or camembert, velvet skin on the outside, creamy aromas, soft consistency. A Comte, young Gouda,
Pilsner beer, Pilsner Urquell, ... the list is huge, but of	Münster with the typical red smear, Romadur, Limburger, a Morbier

course your favorite Pilsner should work for as you know its character if it has a certain hop-bitterness to it!	would also be a good choice.
Alt beer style, Leffe Brune, Nut Brown, Amber Ale, Helles Bock, Pale Ale, … We now enter the stronger, sometimes a little sweeter and smoother beer styles with more complex mouthfeel	Bergkäse mild (made in mountain regions of Europe), very aromatic and some acidity Camembert, Brie aged, Gouda aged, Morbier, Triple Cream, …
Orval Trappist, Dark wheat, Seasonal Specials, Bock beer, … More alcohol and a more complex mouthfeel	Triple Cream, Comte, mature goat cheese (in ash), nice and light inside and gray outside with some noble, mould earthy, with the typical taste and smell. Mountain cheese strong, nutty, smelling of hay. Smoked mozzarella, …

Hoppy beers, India Pale Ale (IPA), Imperial or double IPA, Duvel, .. Crisp and complex hoppy aromas and a maybe a challenge for your mouth and nose	Parmesano Reggiano, Sharp Cheddar, Grande Padano, Sbrinz, Ädelost, …
Triple Maredsous, Quadruple La Trappe. There is also a large selection of strong beers around the world, but they should not be bitter or brewed with roasted malt. These beers are well over 8% to 12% alc. by Vol. Imperial Stout, Barley Wine, Doppelbock, … Creamy crown, smooth mouthfeel, …	Blue Stilton, Cambozola, Roquefort, Bavaria Blu, Bleu d'Auvergne, Old Sarum, …

When browsing through these combinations you will find that the order always changes a little. Don't worry; it is completely permissible and is an essential part of the "experiment".

Let it sink in and you will see, it always starts with a light beer and a light cheese and ends with the powerful aromas and flavours.

Craft beer – special beers – and more!

Pairing craft beers with cheese is difficult in my opinion, because every brewery brews with different yeast strains, temperatures, malts and hops, which results in very individual and wonderful beers. As always: practice!

If we start with the beer in the previous pairings, because the beer is relatively constant in quality and type (variety), we start with the cheese in the craft beer pairings, because this – compared to the craft beers – the "constant" component.

It gets even more difficult when you want to taste cheese from small dairies and combine them with craft beers. But that is exactly what makes it so appealing and you will be amazed at what you will find in your area and what is worth trying.

IPA (India Pale Ale) heavily hopped and not for every palate, especially not if it is a "Double IPA".
My favourite hops: Magnum, Cascade, Hallertauer, Cirtrus, Saazer.

A spicy cheddar or a slightly sharp feta goes well with the IPA, as these harmonize with the intense hop aroma.

When buying beer, please check the label. Often the beer colour is already given in EBC (colour) and the hop bitterness in IBU (bitterness).

If you are shopping in a brewery, ask the staff, they are trained and are happy to provide information. The Internet is also a good source, but be careful with forums, as all kinds of "cheese" are published there.

Seasonal- and Christmas beer styles!

Many breweries produce Märzen for the spring and a beer brewed with spices and herbs for the winter. The Märzen often has a slightly stronger colour and is very tasty.

The Christmas beer brewed in Germany, with spices or herbs, is often called "brewing speciality" because according to the German beer law it is no longer beer. Outside of Germany this is not valid.
In my opinion, all strong cheeses with spices go well with this, of course Christmas cookies with cinnamon, coriander, brown sugar, and the gingerbread is a must.

The **Rauchbier**, the speciality from Bamberg/ Germany is almost a meal by itself. Dark, rich, full of flavour. I could hardly drink the first glass, let alone enjoying it.
BUT, this stuff is great and once you get the taste, the flavour, it's an experience. Honestly! Depending on how smoky it is for your taste buds, I would try a smoked mozzarella or a cheese that comes with ham, nuts, or diced bacon.
Sauerbiere: especially made with sour beer components it tastes good with mature, complex cheese. It is also popular as an aperitif.

There are always exceptions to what I propose here. So be gracious!

The Hanse-Porter from Störtebecker, for example, brewed with caramel malts, also goes wonderfully with a chocolate cake because it has less alcohol than other porters and is very sweet in taste. The recommended drinking temperature here is 16 °.

By the way, our neighbours also make great beers. For example, I discovered excellent Polish beers that shimmer golden yellow and taste very aromatic – with an aged Gouda or a Munster.

Every country has its own beer-style and you will find more and more Craft breweries all around the world.

Salad from "Limburger" or "Romadur"

The dressing first. In a bowl add 3-4 table-spoons granola oil or a light olive oil, 1-2 table-spoons white wine vinegar, a pinch of salt and sugar, add white ground pepper. Stir together with 2 tablespoons of finely chopped onion.

The cheese (200-250g for 2 people, approx. 1 cup for 2 people) cut in thin slices and immediately place it into the dressing otherwise the slices may stick together. Stir.
Sprinkle with parsley and serve it with a French bread or a sour dough bread, even a pretzel would work.

You can also place the slices on a plate and then sprinkle parsley and the dressing on top.

With the right temperature you may have to let some fresh air in your kitchen.

Beer choice:
Märzen, Oktoberfest beer, Wheat

**French bread (Baguette) topped/ gratin-
ated with cheese**

Cut the bread lengthwise or in 1-inch thick slices, add butter or olive oil and roast it on the BBQ, in a non-stick pan or under the broiler for a few minutes.

Add the cheese. Use goat cheese, Brie, Gouda Munster or Roquefort.

Bake or broil it again for a few minutes and make sure you do not burn the cheese.
Please let it cool down because hot melted cheese is not pleasure if it sticks to your palate.

Beer choice:
According to the cheese you add to the bread you know already what would fit your taste.

Cheese-and-pear relish

peel the pears and cut into small pieces, add walnut oil, diced shallot, roast the caraway and coriander seeds in the pan, but do not burn, grind, add to the pan with the pears, deglaze with the juice of an orange.
Cut the Gouda into bites, but not too small and serve with the relish, done.

Cheese variations a bit different

Try a Brie and/or Camembert with Dijon mustard, a Mozzarella with a Crema di Balsamico, a goat cheese with black olives and a Romadur with a Mango Crema di Balsamico ...

Be creative!

There are a few things to be considered!

As with any tasting, I would like to point out that perfume, tobacco smoke, garlic, spicy food, etc. can affect the experience.

If you are pregnant or have problems with alcohol this Tasting should be a NO-GO.
Raw milk cheese is not recommended for pregnant women. Please seek medical advice or ask your doctor before you eat raw milk cheese.

Attention: After the tasting you have approx. 6×0.1 litre / approx. 20 ounces of beer consumed.
Do not drink and drive!
Driving or motorcycling is a no-go! ... and even walking and cycling can be dangerous. Do not operate any machinery.

Do something good for yourself and your guests, try something new. Even if beer was once the drink of the poor people, its image and quality provide us with more than just a drink, a great beer is a luxury item.

Cheese has a long tradition, and it is just not possible to research when men started to make and eat cheese. The number of types of cheese is huge. So, enjoy the idea, be amazed, be creative, have fun tasting.

The brewers, cheesemakers and affineurs do a great job a deserve applause. I appreciate what they do very much and I want to try something new right now.

This book about beer and cheese is intended to awaken a passion in you, inspire you, cheer you on and ... your creativity.

Use this guide as a business idea. Why not? Transform it, use it, enjoy it.

Just a while ago I was listening to Vivaldi's "four seasons". What if you find 4 chesses that would represent the four seasons in your area and find 4 beers to accommodate the cheese?!

Use the details of taste, aroma and art of mak-
ing given to entertain your guests.

Cheers to you and your guests!

Sincerely, Harald Müller

A small index:

A   Affineur, Affinage, refining cheese

B   Bock, usually *a dark lager*

C   Craft-Bier, traditional hand-crafted and
         generally made with traditional ingredi-
         ents

D   Doppelbock, deep gold to dark brown,
         with a large, creamy, persistent head
         and a strong malty aroma and a high
         original gravity

E   EBC = European Brewery Convention
         (Wikipedia EBC Beer) controls the col-
         our of beer. It is controlled by how
         much light is absorbed..

         Enzyme, (Beer) – Molecules that help to
         extract the sugar molecules from the
         starch to be converted in to alcohol.

         Enzyme, (Cheese) – pepsin similar to
         chymosin in clotting milk substrate
         with respect to the influence of pH.

F   Fermentation, (Beer) a process where sugar is converted in to alcohol.

G   Gravity (see Original Gravity)

H

I   IPA – India Pale Ale, a hoppy beer style within the broader category of pale ale. and would grow in popularity, notably as an export beer shipped to India and elsewhere

         IBU – International Bitter Units,

J

K   Kriek – Belgium Cherry beer

L   Lager, The primary definition of a lager is that it is a bottom-fermented beer

M   Malt, germinated grain that has been dried in a process known as "malting"

         Maltose – Maltose, also known as maltobiose or malt sugar

Mouthfeel, textural attributes of beer, those which produce a tactile feeling in the mouth

N

O   Original Gravity, a measure of the solids content origin ally in the wort, before alcoholic fermentation has star ted

P   Plato, is used to quantify the concentration of extract, mainly sugars, derived from malt

Q

R

S   Sommelier, someone who serves and gives advice about beer or wine.

Stout, dark beer, often brewed with roasted malt to extract colour and roast aroma.

T

U umami – essence of deliciousness" in Japanese, and its taste is often described as the meaty, savoury deliciousness of food.

V
W Witbeer - Belgium beer, (usually top fermented)

   Weizenbier, Hefeweizen - Wheat beer

X

Y Yeast, fermentation, yeast cells convert cereal-derived sugars. It also influences the aroma and taste of beer.

Z

Notes:

About me:

In my real life I make a living as an IT-Consultant and in my spare time I ran my own side business as a personal coach. Home-brewing fills the gap between other things. In 1994 I brewed my first own beer. 20 bottles "Helles", a Pale Ale with approx. 6% Alc.
The first brewing was a rather exiting process, the drinking process was a fun event with some brave pals at the table who gave their very best.
My first home-brewed beer was not cold filtered and had a very wild aroma and "rustic" taste. Still, it was a good start and after a few more procedures I succeeded in taste and less strange facial expressions. At that time the terms "Micro brews" and "Craft Beer" had not entered my vocabulary.

1996 I moved to Oregon to work for a small company and enjoyed 5 years there. In Oregon I discovered the Micro Brews. Amazing! I am still a fan of McMenamins, Deschutes, Rogue and many many more.

When I was living in Salem, Oregon there have been 4 Micro brews and Pubs and one shop where you could buy all the equipment and ingredients to brew your own beer. The name: „Home Brew Heaven "! Any questions?

When I started as a home brewer, we had only a few new breweries here in Germany. Today the Brewing culture is a vital part not only in European countries but also around the world and many of the beers are available in almost any corner of the globe. In any country there are the big Breweries but there are more and more small craft breweries too.
Great Pale Ales excellent Wheat Beer, IPA, and Imperial Stout, just to name a few, they are out there to discover.

The brewers are brave and daring and successful!
For us as customers and beer lovers a good thing. Go out, discover, enjoy, share, dare, trust, and have a great time!

Thanks!

To all who helped and contributed in any way to make this book possible!

To all who provided their opinion while tasting my home brewed beer.

To all who attended my tastings and who have been very patiently with me.

References:
(at the time when this book is published)
„Cheese & Beer", Janett Fletcher
„Tasting Beer", Randy Mosher
„Käse der Welt", Juliet Harbutt
„Handbuch Käse", Komet Verlag Köln
„Der Zoigl", Wolfgang Benkhardt
„Der Geschmack des Weins", DVD, tricast Team Wuppertal
„Käse" von Leonie Class
„Das kleine Bierquiz", Huch&Friends
„Heimbrauen für Fortgeschrittene" Hagen Rudolph, Verlag Hans Carl
„Bierbrauen für jedermann" Michael Hlatky, Franz Reil, Leopold Stocker Verlag
„Der Zoigl" Wolfgang Benkhardt, Buch & Kunstverlag Oberpfalz
„Bier Guide" Sünje Nicolaysen, Heyne
„Bier-Aroma-Guide" Fachverlag Hans Carl
„Wikipedia "
https://www.dictindustry.de